CHILDREN OF THE WILD

CAN YOU IMAGINE what it would be like to be lost in the woods and not be rescued for years? Could you stay alive? There have been many cases of children who survived alone in the wilderness for years. Many of these stories tell of these children being taken care of by wild animals—the boy raised by gazelles in the Sahara; Parasram, the wolf boy of Agra; Amala and Kamala, the girls raised in a wolf den; and many more. Since it is not uncommon for a human to care for a hurt or lost baby animal, why should it be so strange for an animal to care for a lost human child? Think about this, and then let your imagination go as you read these incredible stories. Some of these tales are only partly true; some may be entirely true; a few show how ordinary incidents can be turned into a "wolf child" story; and some are purely fiction. Whatever they may be, all the stories tell of the common bond between people and animals and show that, indeed, truth may be stranger than fiction.

CHILDREN
of the WILD

JOHN R. BURGER
and
LEWIS GARDNER

Photographs

JULIAN MESSNER   New York

Published by Julian Messner,
A Simon & Schuster Division of
Gulf & Western Corporation,
Simon & Schuster Building,
1230 Avenue of the Americas,
New York, New York 10020.
Second Printing, 1979
Designed by Irving Perkins
Manufactured in the United States of America

Library of Congress Cataloging in Publication Data

Burger, John R
  Children of the wild.

  Bibliography: p. 121
  Includes index.
  SUMMARY: A collection of true stories and legends about
children who were raised by animals.
  1. Wolf children—Juvenile literature. [1. Wolf children]
I. Gardner, Lewis, joint author.   II. Title.
GN372.B87   155.4'5'67   78-4627
ISBN 0-671-32879-4

Contents

CHAPTER ONE

The Gazelle Boy of the Sahara

HE WAS TRAVELING through the western part of the Sahara, the great desert of North Africa. He was alone, riding a camel through a landscape of sand dunes and splintered rock. The heat seemed to draw the moisture from his bones. In this land of mirages, a man might not believe what he saw with his own eyes.

And he had reason to doubt his eyes. In a herd of gazelles that were running lightly over the plain, he saw something unbelievable. Gazelles are a kind of small, swift antelope. They were not unusual in that part of the desert, but running among them seemed to be a boy —a human child!

He ran with the same speed and graceful movements as the rest of the herd. But he ran on two legs instead of four. He was not running *after* the animals; he was running *with* them as part of the herd.

Suddenly, both boy and animals were gone.

Could this have been a genie of the desert, one of the strange and mischievous spirits the nomads spoke about? Last night at the campfire, he had heard a tale of a child that had grown up with ostriches. It ate the same food as they did and could run just as fast. The storyteller promised him that within a day's journey he would find an even greater surprise.

Now, here it was. Was this a real boy living as a gazelle or some strange desert illusion? Advancing to the point where the herd had disappeared, he found hoofprints in the sand. Among them were small human footprints. It was a real boy, after all.

But how did he get here? How did he survive? Did he know he was something other than just another gazelle?

The man followed the tracks in the sand through the growing heat of the day. He kept on the trail with only a handful of dates and a swallow of water to keep up his strength. The tracks led to a small oasis in the side of an isolated, flat-topped mountain. Here there were bushes and a few trees for the animals' food and shade. But most important, there was water. This seemed to be the herd's headquarters and hiding place.

It was here, watching from a distance, that he got his first good look at the gazelle boy. When the boy ran, his long black hair flew behind him like a horse's mane. His eyes were dark brown and almond-shaped. The expression on his face was open and serene. His body was deeply tanned and crisscrossed with numerous scars. The scars suggested that life in the wild was not easy.

The man, Jean-Claude Armen, knew that capturing the boy would make it impossible to study how he lived. Nor could he sneak up on the boy and the herd in a place where there was little to hide behind. A slight shift in the wind would bring his scent to their sensitive nostrils. They would run away in a panic. If he made any noise, this too would scare them away.

The only hope was to be accepted by the herd as an animal that was harmless to them. The best way to do this was to approach them carefully, without sudden movement, but not getting too close. Then he would sit still and wait for the boy and the animals to get used to him.

After five days of waiting, one of the youngest and most curious of the gazelles was attracted to the stranger. The young gazelle's curiosity overcame its caution. It came close enough to sniff the man's toe. When nothing frightening happened, it sniffed again. Then it licked the toe.

This was the beginning of Armen's acceptance by the gazelles. In time, the rest of the herd approached, sniffed, and then licked his toe or hands. The boy, too, went through this ritual of acceptance.

Armen stayed with the herd for several weeks. He learned a good deal about the boy's place in the animals' world.

At first glance, the boy seemed to be a free child of nature. But it soon became clear to Armen that the animals had rules that bound the boy more tightly than any human etiquette. If he broke the rules, the relentless forces of nature would punish him.

Food was the first concern of the herd. The younger members of the herd acted as scouts. They would leave the group and hunt for places where food was growing. It might be bushes or low tree limbs, or the small, short-lived desert plants that spring up and die in a few hours.

When one of the scouts found food, he returned to the herd to tell them how to get to it. The scout went to the leader of the herd. He stamped his hooves and pointed with his body, to show in what direction the food could be found. Armen believed that the number of times the gazelle stamped told the leader how far away the food was. The leader would then tell the other members of the herd how far and in what direction the food lay. Then they would all move off in that direction for their next meal.

Most of the time, the boy lived on the same diet of plants as the gazelles. When food became really scarce, he would also eat lizards.

Although the boy often walked on all fours, he had some characteristics that could be considered "human."

One of these Armen discovered in an experiment. He took a pile of twigs and lit them with a match. The boy was interested in the strange new red flower—the flames from the burning wood. He came closer and closer. Then he grabbed a fistful of embers. He held them without any show of pain, probably because of the calluses on his palm.

When Armen first saw the boy, he was about ten years old. Armen concluded that he had joined the herd at a very early age, perhaps as young as five to seven months.

The boy would not have been able to live on plants or lizards at that tender age. But there was an old female gazelle that the boy seemed very fond of. Armen wondered if perhaps when the boy was a baby—lost by a family of nomads crossing the desert—the female gazelle had nursed him. Her milk would have kept him alive.

Armen's reconstruction of the gazelle boy's beginnings is very much like the story in American folklore about Pecos Bill. Instead of falling out of a basket slung on the side of a camel, Pecos Bill fell out of the covered wagon that was bringing his parents westward. The infant Bill was adopted and reared by a family of coyotes. He later rejoined human society and was known for his wild exploits in the Old West. But the stories were never supposed to be true.

Jean-Claude Armen is a poet and painter. He has

traveled a great deal to interesting places. But here, in the Sahara, meeting and watching the gazelle boy moved him more than anything else.

Armen was finally forced by time and lack of supplies to leave the desert and return to France. He studied what had been written about wild children.

Until then, he had thought of them as poetic images of freedom. But he learned that, compared to ordinary children, they were mentally retarded. A child that grows up in the wild will probably never learn to talk, even if put in the hands of kind and expert teachers.

Armen left the desert in 1961. In 1963 he returned. His goal was to find the boy and the herd in the Spanish Sahara. The first time, he had entered from Mauritania in the south. This second time, he entered from Morocco in the north.

Since even a small expedition is very expensive, he was pleased when a captain of the French Army in Morocco offered to help. He provided a jeep for himself, Armen, and another officer.

The roar of the engine filled the desert air. Armen recognized landmarks close to the herd's oasis hiding place. He worried if the boy was still alive.

On the previous trip, he had left the herd for two days. On his return, he had been greeted with affection. What a greeting it would be after an absence of two years! The soldiers would be surprised to see their companion surrounded by a friendly herd of gazelles, with the wild boy among them.

After leaving the jeep and the officers at a distance to watch through binoculars, Armen approached the oasis on foot. The herd, though changed, was still there. The young animals had grown up. The boy's gazelle foster-mother was gone. Perhaps she had been shot by a hunter or killed by a jackal. The boy was there. He looked stronger and more mature.

It was a sad reunion. The animals did not recognize him. Even more disturbing, the boy didn't remember him.

Armen had to start all over again. But this time, he knew how to communicate with the animals. He was soon accepted by the herd once more.

After a few days of study, the men had to return to civilization. Armen watched the boy from the jeep with the officers. The sun was setting. Suddenly the captain decided to see how fast the boy could run. He stepped on the gas and started chasing him. Armen objected, but the captain kept his foot to the floor.

They jolted along over the desert, clinging to their vehicle to keep from being bounced out onto the sand and rocks. The herd ran in panic, zigzagging to evade the monster that was roaring after them. Soon they were herded into a steep-sided ravine. The animals couldn't dodge. They had to run straight ahead.

The boy was running with giant leaps, his brown eyes full of fear, as the car gained on him. When they caught up with him, he was running at a speed of 52–54 km/hr (about 33 mph). Then the jeep got a flat tire, and the three men were thrown out onto the ground.

Night was coming on fast. The boy would be able to get away. The tire was changed, and the captain tried again to capture the boy. This time Armen succeeded in getting control of the jeep. Night fell, and the boy was safe.

Armen felt a deep sadness at leaving the child in this manner, with the vision of a desperate flight—"beautiful nonetheless, almost unreal"—into the vastness of the desert. The adventure was over.

The boy had proved his ability to escape from the most dangerous of his enemies—man. He was to prove this ability again.

Another group tried to capture him. This time they were American military officers. They used two helicopters with a net strung between them. The boy escaped even these modern marvels of civilized engineering.

For all Armen knows, the boy may still be living in the desert, certain that he is a gazelle and happier than he could ever be as a scientific curiosity or a resident in a school for the mentally defective.

Children that grow up in the wild—if they are lost or abandoned at a very early age—can never catch up with children reared in society. In some ways it may be kinder to leave them in the wild, protected as endangered species are.

Armen may have been moved by his own longing for the state of wild freedom that the boy seemed to be living in—a child that didn't need other people, with a perfect body clothed only in the natural dignity of a wild animal.

But what about the boy's constant, desperate search for food in a brutal landscape? What about the need to escape enemies? And should one regret the human characteristics that will never develop?

CHAPTER TWO

What Are Wild Children?

WHAT IF YOU WERE LOST in the woods, so lost that you couldn't find your way out or be rescued for years? How would you stay alive? You would have to find your own food. There would probably be wild animals to avoid. Think, moreover, of getting lost like this at the age of two or three.

There have been cases of children who survived alone in the wilderness for years. In some of these cases, it has been claimed that the children not only were safe among wild animals, they were even adopted by them. There are many stories of children being adopted by wolves, bears, and other animals, including, of course, gazelles. How many of these stories are true?

Just suppose a young child is lost in the woods. He or

17

she has a chance of surviving by eating wild herbs, fruit, and roots, and by catching small animals or birds. This has happened. Reliable accounts of this sort of survival are described in this book.

Furthermore, what if a lost infant encounters a wolf? And the wolf, instead of attacking the child, nuzzles at it like a big friendly dog, licks the grimy, tear-stained face, and then gently grasps the child in its jaws and carries it off to its warm den to bring it up with its own cubs. What a wonderful picture of "human" kindness being shown by a wild animal!

From the beginning of history—and before—people have had close associations with animals. We have hunted them, bred them for milk and meat production, and tamed them to work for us and be our companions. Myth and folklore are full of stories of talking animals, gods that disguise themselves as animals, and animals that are really people that have been put under a spell. Because we think we know animals so well, we see human characteristics in them. They may seem happy or sad, clever or dull, and may even appear to have a sense of humor. Similarly, we see animal characteristics in people. A person can be strong as a bull, brave as a lion, clever as a fox, or dirty as a pig.

It is not uncommon for a human to care for a hurt or lost baby animal, like a bird that has a broken wing or a baby raccoon that has lost its mother. Why should it be so strange for an animal to care for a lost human child?

What Are Wild Children?

Some of the earliest myths show animals adopting human infants. One example is the story of Romulus and Remus, the founders of Rome. In the myth, they are set out in the wilderness to die while they are babies. A she-wolf suckles them and saves their lives.

There are two threads that run through this book. One is that there is a kinship between people and animals. The other is that determining the truth of a "true" story can be very difficult. Honest people seeing the same event can all tell different stories, being sure that they all are telling the truth. If you add a little self-interest

Romulus and Remus (*N. Y. Public Library Picture Collection*)

or yarn-spinning, simple reporting rapidly becomes fiction. In time, perhaps, it will become folklore.

In the case of children who have lived in the wild—or, as they are often called, feral children—there are few or no reliable witnesses of their life in the wild. So the truth is very hard, if not impossible, to determine. Sometimes the best that can be done is to put together all the evidence about a case, and then decide what seems probable.

Sometimes it seems likely that only parts of some of the "true" stories are true. Some of them may be true all the way through. A few stories are included in this book because they show how a rather ordinary incident can be turned into a "wolf child" story, even though it turns out there never *was* a wolf.

The purpose of this book is to entertain and inform. It is a blend of materials. Some of the stories are true, some are fiction, and some are a combination of the two. We have done our best to indicate which are which.

In the past few years millions of people have been exposed to the idea of wild children. There have been television series like "Mary Hartman, Mary Hartman" with its character Johnny Doe, a wild child who was raised by Bigfoot; television movies like *Stalk the Wild Child;* a series, "Lucan"; and the movie *Mara of the Wilderness.* An important reason for the recent popularity of this theme was a film made by François

Truffaut, the French movie director. His film was called *L'Enfant Sauvage* (*The Wild Child*). Of course, there were wild children in movies and fiction long before Truffaut, such as *Tarzan of the Apes* and Mowgli, the wolf boy in Kipling's *Jungle Books.* But *The Wild Child* is important because it was meant to be an accurate presentation of the true case of Victor, the wild boy of Aveyron.

There can be no reasonable doubt that there have been children like Victor of Aveyron who have survived on their own in the wild. But more appealing still are the cases where it is claimed that the children grew up with wild animals. Not only grew up with them, but learned some of their skills, acquired some of their strength, and learned their language.

The rest of this book will try to tell what real wild children are like and how they survived. Have children really lived with animals? What are some of the made-up stories about wild children? What can wild children teach us about animals and about ourselves?

CHAPTER THREE

Wild Children of Europe

THE STORY OF CHILDREN of the wild as we know them begins in Europe. Over the years, especially during times of great chaos and confusion—as when the countryside was ravaged by war or disease—young children got lost or their parents were killed and they were left alone. Once they were alone, they lived or died depending upon their age, their health, their adaptability to circumstances, and their luck.

Most of them probably died. A few of them survived in the wild. There were many claims that they survived because they were adopted by wild animals. There are older stories in myth as well.

There are also many stories from historical times. This chapter relates some of the stories that led early scientists to conclude that there was a subspecies of man known as *Homo sapiens ferus,* or wild man. In fact, these were individual wild humans and not a separate variety. According to one respected biologist of the eighteenth century, all these wild humans had three things in common: they were mute (did not talk), they walked on all fours, and their bodies were covered with hair.

Some of the stories of wild children are rather silly, and a reader must judge whether they seem true or even likely. In one case it was claimed that wolves brought up a boy and gave him the best part of their kill. They covered him with leaves at night to keep him warm. They also taught him how to run on all fours as swiftly as a wolf.

One of the true and better known cases was that of Wild Peter of Hameln. Long after he became famous, it was learned that he was the son of a Mr. Krüger. Mr. Krüger had a problem taking care of the boy himself after his wife died. The boy was unable to speak properly and was difficult to control. In 1723 he ran away.

A year later, the boy turned up in a distant village. He was sent back to his father. Meanwhile, Krüger had married again. His new wife must not have gotten along with her strange stepson, because he was thrown out of the house and never returned to it.

How could his parents in their German village imagine that their mute son would die in England sixty-two years later, after living on a pension given to him by George I, king of England?

The boy was about twelve years old when he left home for the last time. His story continues in the town of Hameln, which is also famous for the story of the Pied Piper. On July 27, 1724, the boy was seen in a field near the town. He was naked and tanned brown by the sun. Using apples for bait, a man lured him into town and captured him. The children of the town made fun of him. They probably would have hurt him by throwing stones at him if adults had not interfered. One thing the children did was to name him Peter. After that, he was called Wild Peter of Hameln.

Peter tried to escape, but failed. He was filthy and had terrible table manners. His favorite food at this time was fresh bark peeled from sticks. He also liked various vegetables, especially onions. Whenever he was given anything to eat, he would first smell it carefully. Then he would eat it or not, depending on the smell. Like other wild children, he was very good at catching birds for food.

At this time George I was king of England. George was a German by birth and kept close ties with Germany. He had heard about Wild Peter and, believing he was a true example of primitive man, wanted to find out what he was like.

The intellectuals of Europe had been discussing what kind of ideas would be found in a mind that had not been affected by education or by dealings with other

Wild Peter of Hameln (*Blumenbach's* Beytrage zur
Naturgeschichte)

people. Peter seemed to be a heaven-sent way to settle
the question. So King George had Peter brought to
England.

Peter disappointed the British scientists. They decided he was only an idiot. He was sent off to be cared
for on a farm.

Peter never learned to speak properly. This got him
into trouble once when he wandered far from the farm.

When people asked him who he was or where he was going, he could not answer.

At that time there was political trouble in England. People believed that spies for a rival to the throne were at large in the countryside. Peter was thrown into jail on suspicion of being a spy. That night there was a fire, and the cells were unlocked to let the prisoners get away from the flames. When the jailkeeper counted his prisoners, he found that Peter was missing. He went back through clouds of smoke to find Peter in his cell. He seemed to be enjoying the excitement of the fire. Peter was led to safety. Eventually the prison authorities learned who Peter was, and he was returned to the farm where he belonged.

Peter had had his time as a celebrity in London. He was mentioned in many scientific reports on natural man.

Many fanciful stories grew up about him. One claimed that he had been found by King George while hunting; another that his body was covered with hair and that he moved about on all fours. According to another story, he learned to speak in nine months. None of these were true. He was just a boy who was turned away from his home and turned wild to survive. By chance, he was saved and considered a sort of original savage man. He lived on to old age on the farm in England.

A case of a wild child who was the result of the disruption caused by war was Jean of Liège. Soldiers were plundering his village in the Ardennes region of France.

To escape them, he fled to the woods. From the age of five years to sixteen, he was said to have lived in the woods by eating acorns and wild fruit and herbs. When he returned to live among people again, he longed to go back to his old life in the forest.

While in the forest and for a while after leaving it, his sense of smell became highly developed. He was able to tell one wild food from another by its smell. He could also, from some distance, identify by smell the woman who took care of him.

An Irish sheep boy comes into the records when he is described in 1672 by the noted Dr. Tulp, who appears in Rembrandt's famous painting *Dr. Tulp's Anatomy Lesson.*

The boy was about sixteen years old. He had escaped from his parents in Ireland and lived among sheep from a very early age. He had supposedly taken on some of their habits. He ate grass and hay, smelling everything carefully before eating it. And he bleated.

Dr. Tulp may have seen the boy when he was brought to Amsterdam as part of a show. This possibility should not inspire great confidence in his being a real wild child. Even today, carnivals display fraudulent wild men to amaze the public.

There are stories from the seventeenth century of boys being raised by bears in Lithuania. One version

Artist's conception of the Bear-boy of Lithuania

takes place around 1657, when a boy was "found among bears" and captured. He was given the name of Joseph. When found, he went on all fours and made bearlike noises. He did not want to wear either clothes or shoes. Although he was eventually taught to walk upright, he seemed to walk more like a trained bear than a human child.

There were many scars on his body, supposedly caused by the bears. His preferred foods were raw vegetables and raw meat.

There is a case of a "bear girl" of Hungary. In 1767 she was found in a cave by hunters who had been chasing a bear. There is no evidence—besides her living in the cave—that she had anything to do with bears. She was tall and strong and about eighteen years of age. Although she was clearly very much afraid of the hunters, she did not cry when they captured her and took her back to civilization. She was locked up in the town. She ate raw meat and wild roots and tree bark.

Another supposed wild girl was caught in 1717 in Cranenburg in the Netherlands. This girl, too, was about eighteen. She was said to have been kidnapped at the age of sixteen months by a woman who had lost her baby and needed a child in order to receive an inheritance. Once she got the money, she turned the child loose. The girl had lived on grass and plants.

After many years the girl was trapped in nets by a large group of farmers who had been sent after her. The girl and her mother were reunited. Unlike what happens in most of these stories, they not only recognized each other, but were happy to be together again.

When the girl was captured, she had thick, matted hair and very dark skin. According to an early account, her dark skin peeled off, revealing light skin underneath. This probably means that the covering of dirt on her skin came off when she was washed. The girl had a pleasant disposition and liked to laugh. The account ends by saying that she was beginning to learn to talk.

One of the most charming cases was a girl who was called Mlle. le Blanc, or Miss White. She turned up one fall evening in 1731, in a village of the Champagne district of France. She was nine or ten years old and dressed in rags and animal skins. She came into the village to get a drink of water. She carried a club with her. When a dog attacked her, she killed it with one bash on the head and jumped up and down on its body for joy. After her victory she climbed a tree and went to sleep. She was soon caught by the villagers and brought to the local castle.

While she was there, she saw a cook cleaning a bird for cooking. She took the bird and started eating it.

Someone, probably feeling sorry for the poor little girl, gave her a little rabbit. The kind person probably thought it would make her happy to have a little pet. It *did* make her happy—she strangled it and then ate it.

The girl could swing from the branches of one tree to the branches of another. She could also swim and dive so well that she could catch fish and frogs for food.

When she later learned to talk, she revealed that at first she had had another girl as a companion. One day they found a set of rosary beads and quarreled over who should have it. Mlle. le Blanc hit the other girl on the head with a club. When the girl started bleeding and crying, she felt sorry for her. She caught a number of frogs and plastered their skins over the wound. Shortly after this, the girls parted company, with Mlle. le Blanc wearing the rosary as a bracelet.

When first found, she used crying as a sort of speech. It was very disagreeable and made it difficult for people to get along with her. Also disagreeable—and much more dangerous—was the way in which she reacted to anything she thought was a threat. For example, once when she was eating a piece of raw meat, a man approached the child in order to hug her. She smacked him with her hand. He almost fell over from the force of the blow and was temporarily stunned and blinded.

In time, she did learn some manners. When dining at a castle at a large dinner party, she found there was nothing to eat that she liked. She went outside and caught a mess of frogs. Then she distributed them by handfuls to the other guests. Frogs, properly prepared, are, of course, a delicacy. However, completely un-prepared—alive and hopping with fright, in fact—they did not appeal to the other guests. When she saw this, Mlle. le Blanc collected the frogs from their plates.

Her capture in the Champagne district was the second time she was caught, as may be suspected from the fact that she was wearing rags and animal skins. The first time she was in the care of a woman who not only gave her clothes, but also taught her to do needlepoint.

Perhaps she was older than most other wild children when she became lost in the woods. This would mean she had been with humans longer, and might explain why she was one of the few wild children to make significant recovery from the wild state. In any case, she learned to talk. She had some understanding of abstract ideas. She finally became a nun.

It is difficult to decide how much of her story is true —surely some of it is, perhaps all of it is. She was certainly a remarkable creature. She seemed to take fate in her own hands and do something on her own behalf. She was more than just a hapless victim of a deprived environment.

Two other European cases of considerable interest are Victor of Aveyron and Kaspar Hauser. To tell their stories will take chapters of their own.

CHAPTER FOUR

Victor, the Wild Boy of Aveyron

IN THE LAST YEARS of the eighteenth century, a naked boy was seen several times around the forests and farms of southern France. He was captured twice, but he escaped. Villagers saw him eating acorns and roots or potatoes from the fields. Sometimes he would be given food at the farmhouses.

Early in January 1800, when he was around twelve years old, he came to the village of Saint-Sermin in the department of Aveyron. The villagers kept him from escaping. This was the end of his life in the wild.

The year 1800 was a short time after the French Revolution. The revolution had inspired new ways of thinking about politics and society. New ideas were in the air in other fields also, as people tried to use science to conquer superstition and tradition. Some of these new ideas would be tested and developed with this strange boy of the wild.

Several people, including scientists and physicians, were eager to study the boy. This would be a chance to see what people were really like when they lived free of civilization. A French writer of an earlier time, Rousseau, had thought that man in a natural state would be a "noble savage." Many expected the boy from Aveyron to be one. But he appeared to be dirty and disagreeable, less noble than any animal.

A professor of natural history in Aveyron studied the boy and made several observations. The boy had a pleasant smile. His body was covered with scars, probably from burns. He had a long scar on his neck, as if someone had tried to kill him by cutting his throat. He trotted instead of walked. He could hear, although he didn't respond to speech. His senses of smell and taste were very good. The only emotions he seemed to have were concerned with wanting food, enjoying rest, and feeling sad about not being free. He was only interested in people insofar as they were involved in taking care of him.

The boy was sent to the Institute for Deaf-Mutes in Paris. The director of the institute was Roche-Ambroise Sicard, who was interested in anthropology, the study of man. Sicard studied the boy and found he showed little progress in learning anything. He decided the boy was hopelessly retarded.

Jean-Marc-Gaspard Itard, a twenty-six-year-old physician, was a friend of Sicard's. Sicard made Itard the institute's physician. One of his duties was to try to train the wild boy.

In 1801 and 1806, Itard wrote about his experiences with the boy. The detailed reports make interesting reading today. They even inspired François Truffaut's film *The Wild Child*. The methods of instruction Itard developed as he worked with the boy led to many educational practices that we now take for granted.

Itard's new pupil was not a very promising specimen. He could not speak, and his eyes wandered from place to place, not focusing on any object for very long. His sense of touch was so insensitive that he could pull potatoes from a pot of boiling water with no apparent pain. He was indifferent to sounds—including pistol shots and music—unless they were related to food, like the sound of a walnut being cracked.

Itard believed that a person's nature is mostly determined by his education. By education he didn't mean just the time spent in school, but every experience a person has from birth, especially his experiences with other people. He felt that the wild boy, by being abandoned in the woods at an early age, had never had a chance to learn the things that we think make a person human. He now attempted to make up for the boy's loss.

Itard knew that other wild children had been found. He also knew that no one had been able to educate them. He thought they failed because they had tried to use ordinary teaching methods to teach extraordinary children.

Itard's plan was carefully thought out. Parts of the plan were simple things that anyone might think of. But, in fact, they would turn out to be revolutionary ideas in the history of education. For example, the boy would respond better to people if they were kind to him and considerate of his needs and wishes. There were four things he really liked, Itard said in his first report— "sleeping, eating, doing nothing, and running about the fields."

Since the boy liked to sleep, he was put to bed as soon as it was dark. He was given the foods he liked, mostly vegetables. When he didn't want to do anything at all, no one bothered him. Whenever possible, he was taken for walks.

Itard's next step was to increase the sensitivity of the boy's senses and emotions and to create new needs. To make him more sensitive to heat and cold, the boy was kept warmly clothed during the day and well covered when he was in bed at night. He was given long, hot baths.

After three months, the boy was able to tell hot from cold, smooth from rough. Because of his new sensitivity to heat and cold, he began to sneeze and to catch head colds. Touch, taste, and smell developed fairly rapidly. Sight and hearing took longer.

The emotions that the boy showed at first were joy and anger. Itard would sometimes provoke him on purpose, since he had seen that when the boy was angry, he would become better at expressing himself or showing what had bothered him.

Itard once gave him a slight electric shock with a Leyden jar charged with static electricity. Another day, when Itard tried to give him another shock with the jar, the boy cleverly moved Itard's hand so the doctor got the shock instead of him.

At first, Itard tried to interest the boy in playing with toys. But he wasn't interested in them. Itard was, however, successful with games that related to food. He put a shelled walnut under a cup and put two similar but empty cups near it. Then he would move the cups. When the boy could guess correctly which cup had the nut under it, he was given the nut to eat.

The cups were moved slowly at first. After a few successes, the movement was more rapid, requiring more concentration. After a while, the boy enjoyed the game for its own sake. Itard could use inedible objects instead of nuts. The game, of course, had an educational purpose. Itard felt it helped the boy develop attention, judgment, and a steady gaze.

Itard next tried to teach the boy to talk. Part of the

Dr. Itard is gratified when the Wild Child shows signs of becoming civilized. From *The Wild Child* starring Francois Truffaut and Jean-Pierre Cargol. (*United Artists Corp.*)

problem, he suspected, was that people may have to learn to make the basic sounds of human speech by a certain age, or they will never be able to speak. Since the boy didn't have anyone to learn these sounds from in the woods, it might be too late for him to learn them now. But Itard tried to give the boy extra training to compensate for his deprived past.

The boy managed to learn to say "lait" (milk) and "eau" (water), as well as "Oh, Dieu!" (Oh, God!), which Madame Guérin, the woman who took care of him, often said.

Itard let the boy become very thirsty. Then he held a glass of water out to the boy, saying "eau." Then he gave it to another person in the room who said "eau." The boy became frantic, but did not say the word, although he did make a kind of hiss. Rather than torture the boy, Itard gave him a drink.

Itard then tried the word "lait," using a glass of milk. After four days, the boy said "lait" when milk was being poured into his cup.

In as many ways as he could find, Itard tried to lead the boy into speech. He even gave him the name Victor because the boy liked the "o" sound when he heard people using it in conversation. The boy did, in fact, respond to the name when he heard it.

When Victor's senses were fairly well developed, Itard began a process of teaching that he hoped would eventually get Victor to read. First, Victor learned to

match an object—a key or a pair of scissors—with its outline drawn on the wall. Then he hung the object on a
nail under its outline. The objects and their arrange-
ments became increasingly complex.

At first, Victor was able to cope with the new tasks.
But finally a point would be reached at which he would
fail, and he would fall into a rage. From the rage he
would go into a fit like the convulsions of epilepsy.

Itard decided to stop these fits, not by stopping or
changing the lessons, but by shock. He knew that Victor
had a fear of heights. When Victor tried to end a lesson
by throwing a fit, Itard took an extremely dangerous
step. The lesson was being given in a room with a window that opened onto a stone courtyard four floors
below. Itard seized the boy and held him face down
out the window for several seconds. Then he pulled
him back into the room.

From a boy about to have a violent fit, Victor became
pale, was covered with a cold sweat, and trembled. He
went back to his lesson. When the task was completed,
he threw himself on his bed and cried. This was the
first time, as far as Itard knew, that Victor had ever
cried.

Victor was eventually able to spell out the word "lait"
by picking out the correct wooden letters and putting
them in order.

Itard's interest in Victor was partly as a teacher and

a medical man who felt obliged to help the child. But he was also a scientist with an interest in Victor as an exotic specimen. One concern in the scientific world of his day could be phrased this way: How much of what makes up a person is due to heredity, and how much is due to the environment that he grows up in?

The only way to study what a person was like when outside society was by studying children who had been abandoned at an early age to survive on their own. Itard wanted to observe Victor in minute detail and discover —by noting the habits and qualities that Victor lacked —what it is that we owe to our upbringing within society.

This question is still debated today. Itard's conclusion was that when a person grows up in isolation, he or she is inferior to many animals. Life "drags on without intelligence or without feelings, a precarious life reduced to bare animal functions." A human's superiority to animals is due to civilization. "Without civilization, he would be one of the feeblest and least intelligent of animals." His ability to imitate and learn through imitation—particularly to learn to speak—"is very active and energetic during the first years of his life, [but] rapidly wanes with age, with isolation. . . ." + p·37

Five years later, Itard submitted a report on Victor to the Minister of the Interior. Itard had not devoted himself exclusively to the education of Victor during

43

these five years. He was actively working at the Institute for Deaf-Mutes, and he was engaged in his own study and private life. But he did stay interested and active in his attempts to normalize Victor, and he was in daily contact with him.

"To speak of the Wild Boy of Aveyron is to revive a name which now no longer arouses any kind of interest," Itard begins his report. "To be judged fairly," he goes on, "this young man must only be compared with himself." Itard at first had thought that Victor was a normal boy who acted as he did because of his lack of education. He hoped that his special course of education would restore him to normalcy. Itard's course of education did bring about a good deal of progress. But it did not make him normal.

Victor's hearing and speech did not respond well to instruction. Since he would never be able to speak, Itard assumed that he would never learn to understand and communicate abstract ideas. But he was able to do chores. He could shell peas, set the table, and saw wood.

Victor had stayed an essentially selfish person. He would do chores when he enjoyed them, but he would not do anything that required sacrifice or privation. He could, though, respond to affection and to being taken care of.

Toward the end of the second (and last) report, Itard explained that Victor had entered puberty. It caused Victor terrible emotional upset, which he could not understand or control. Itard stated that he had decided not to explain to Victor what was going on, for the sake of decency.

Itard finally stopped trying to educate Victor. The French government continued to pay a woman to take care of him. Someone who visited him ten years after Itard's final report said that Victor was "fearful, half-wild, and unable to learn to speak." Victor died in 1828, when he was in his forties.

Why didn't Victor develop further than he had? Why didn't he learn to speak? Here are some of the possible reasons which students of the subject have suggested:

1. Itard's methods were just not the right ones. If Victor had come along later, when other methods were known, the results might have been better. Or if Itard had been content with teaching Victor to use written symbols—instead of trying to teach him to speak—Victor might have developed further intellectually.

2. The ideal time had passed for Victor to learn the things that children are usually taught during infancy.

3. Victor was brain-damaged or retarded from birth. This is a common explanation for the difficulties wild children have in learning. Yet Victor—and other wild children—have been able to survive in harsh conditions. That takes intelligence.

4. Victor suffered a kind of emotional disturbance called *autism*. Yet the emotional reactions he showed

were generally normal. He did not stay as withdrawn from people as autistic children do. Also, if he was seriously ill emotionally, it would have been harder for him to survive in the wild.

It is, of course, impossible for anyone today to study Victor firsthand. But that is what a modern scientist would need to do in order to decide with certainty which of these explanations—if any—is correct.

As for Victor's teacher, his methods and writings helped make known important new ideas in education, beginning with the needs of the student and finding the best methods to help each student learn. The older method was to assume that there were certain facts that needed to be learned, and the teacher's job was to get every student to learn them.

Itard went on to make important discoveries in teaching deaf children to speak; some of this work was based on his work with Victor. He helped found the field of teaching the mentally retarded. His work also influenced Maria Montessori, one of the most influential thinkers in the field of modern education.

CHAPTER FIVE

Kaspar Hauser

THERE ARE SOME children who are not children of the wild in the sense of growing up in the forest. The wildness of their childhood may be emotional in origin—as with autistic children—or it may even be due to political reasons, as has been suggested in the following case. This story of a young man named Kaspar Hauser is very strange and touching. And it is true.

On May 26, 1828, in the town of Nuremberg in what is now Germany, a young man was seen walking around as if he was drunk. When someone tried to talk with him, it was clear that the boy was unable to speak understandably. Instead, he held out a letter.

The letter was addressed to an army captain who lived nearby. The boy was taken to the captain's house.

He was given meat and beer, but he could not stand even a taste of them. Plain bread and water pleased him most. Since the captain was away, he was taken to the stable, where he soon fell asleep on the straw.

When the captain arrived, he couldn't make any sense of the boy either. He had him sent to the police. The police put him in a tower where they kept vagrants. Once again, the boy fell asleep on a bed of straw.

He had been unable to answer any of the policemen's questions about who he was and where he came from. Someone suggested that maybe he knew how to write. They gave him a pen and ink. Surprisingly, the boy picked up the pen and in a firm hand wrote "Kaspar Hauser."

The letter he carried said that he was being sent by his foster father to be made into a soldier, since his foster father could no longer afford to support him. The letter warned that Kaspar didn't know where he came from, and that it would be useless to try to trace him back to his foster father. According to the note, Kaspar was born in 1812. He was sixteen when he turned up in Nuremberg.

It was true that Kaspar didn't know where he came from. But the letter was probably intended to throw the authorities off the scent. It was written in the style of a semiliterate peasant. Kaspar seemed to be dressed like a peasant. On closer examination, however, most of his clothes were not originally of the sort that a peasant would own. For example, his short jacket had been made of a cut-off frock coat, and his pants were the kind that a footman or a gamekeeper might wear.

Kaspar was 4 feet 9 inches tall. His features and the condition of his body were a strange combination of refinement and brutishness. His face was almost without expression, with his blue eyes fixed straight ahead. But his feet were completely without calluses, and his complexion was clear and light. These features suggested that he was not a peasant and had never worked out of doors. There were vaccination scars on both his arms. At this time, vaccination against smallpox was done only among the upper classes.

He walked like someone who had just learned to walk. He stretched his arms in front of him as he walked along, putting his whole foot down at once, instead of heel first, then toe. He fell often, even walking in his own room. A doctor who examined him thought that his legs showed he had spent a lot of time with his legs stretched out in front of him.

It seemed clear that Kaspar had not spent much time with people. Ordinary things were a source of wonder to him. When he saw a mirror, he tried to find the source of the image behind the glass.

One of the few words he knew was *horse*. But he thought any animal, two-legged or four-legged, was a horse. The "horses" he encountered around Nuremberg included dogs, cats, and geese.

The prison keeper moved Kaspar from the upper part of the tower to the section where the keeper lived with his own family. The keeper's eleven-year-old son and three-year-old daughter would play with this young man of sixteen or seventeen. The boy was probably Kaspar's first real teacher. He taught him to talk. His sister taught Kaspar to string beads.

Kaspar spent a lot of his time with toy horses. When the first one was given to him, he patted it and hung ribbons and strings on its neck. He was soon given other toy horses. He would spend the day trying to feed them and make them drink. He tried not to make the slightest sound as he pushed them across the floor. He was afraid that if he made noise, he would be beaten for it.

He was not, however, afraid of a sword waved near him or a pistol fired in his direction. He did not realize that they could harm him.

Experiments were made in trying to get him to eat meat. Bread was given to him with meat fibers hidden in it. He smelled the bread and did not want to eat it. After persuasion, he ate it and became ill.

As soon as it was dark, he went to sleep. With the first light of day, he woke up. During the day, if curtains were drawn to make the room dark, he would immediately fall asleep.

At first he paid attention only to sounds that directly affected him. Soon he became aware of the other sounds around him. He would become very excited by band music.

It seemed as though his mind and senses were taking in the world around him at an increasingly rapid rate.

Sensations and information were flooding in on him.

After Kaspar had been in Nuremberg for a month, he was visited by Anselm von Feuerbach, a judge. Feuerbach took a lasting interest in Kaspar from a humanitarian and a legal point of view. He published a book in 1832 that gives most of the facts about Kaspar that are mentioned in this chapter.

During his first visit, Feuerbach noticed that a great many toys—horses, lead soldiers, wooden dogs, and the like—were in Kaspar's room, but he was not paying as much attention to them as he had been said to earlier. Perhaps as Kaspar's mind grew in experience, he wanted more stimulating material to work with. His face changed, too. People noticed that it was becoming more alert and more expressive.

To pass the time, Kaspar was busy writing, drawing, and learning about the new world that he found himself in. There were many things in this new world that disturbed him.

One time he saw a large crucifix on the outside of a church. He begged that the man being tortured be taken down from the cross. He thought a statue that he saw in a garden on a rainy day was real; he thought it was funny that the man didn't have the sense to stay where it was dry.

His ignorance and confusion so bothered him that he wished he was back with "the man with whom he had always been." This man is important to Kaspar's story. Kaspar had never known the man's name. But as Kaspar learned to talk, he was able to describe his life before he came to Nuremberg.

As long as he could remember, he had lived in a small, dark, silent room. It was a kind of cage. He was barefoot. He could never tell if it was night or day. He would sit on the floor with his legs stretched out in front of him. He even slept in that position.

When he woke from sleeping, he would find a loaf of bread and a pitcher of water beside him. Sometimes the water would not taste right. When it tasted strange, he would fall into a very deep sleep. When he woke from this deep sleep, he would find that he was wearing clean clothes and that someone had trimmed his fingernails.

In Nuremberg, someone gave Kaspar some water with a drop of opium in it. Kaspar said that it tasted like the water that had put him to sleep.

Shortly before Kaspar found himself in Nuremberg, the man brought a small table to the cage, along with paper and pencil. He did not let Kaspar see his face. He stood behind Kaspar, guiding his hand in the formation of letters on paper. Kaspar was very pleased with this activity. He practiced it over and over. This was how he learned to write his name and a few other words. Until now, the only amusement Kaspar had had was playing with two toy horses.

After the writing lessons had gone on for a while, there were standing lessons. This was a strange and painful activity for someone who had done nothing but sit on the floor for years. Then came walking lessons.

Finally, Kaspar was dressed in fresh clothes. Boots were put on his feet. After this, he remembered a lot of painful walking. As far as he knew, he had walked to Nuremberg. But he may have been drugged and put in a coach to travel part of the way.

Judge Feuerbach was interested in the criminal aspect of the boy's confinement. Whoever had kept the boy in his small room or cage was guilty of illegal imprisonment and ill-treatment. There was also the crime of exposure. Since Kaspar's mind had been kept in an infantile state, he was in danger when he was turned loose in Nuremberg. He could easily have stumbled in front of a carriage or fallen into the river near where he was found.

There was also the cruelty of depriving him of a large part of his life, his childhood. But this did not seem to concern Kaspar too much. He did not feel he had been treated badly. Only once had the man beaten him—when he had been playing too loudly with his horses.

Kaspar's life might have gone on in a fairly normal fashion if he had not decided to write down the story of his life—his memoirs. It became widely known that he was working at this task. What he was putting down was not very significant, but the press and the public didn't know that.

Kaspar's status as a celebrity of Nuremberg became

Kaspar Hauser (*N. Y. Public Library Picture Collection*)

too much for him. His new life—with the constant bombardment of new sensations and the visits of curious people—wore him out. So he would not be injured by all this nervous excitement, he was given into the care of Mr. Daumer, a teacher in the local school. He moved from the town jail to the house of Mr. Daumer and his mother and sister. A public announcement was made that the boy was to be left alone or the police would remove unwelcome visitors.

When Kaspar moved into his new home and slept in a real bed for the first time, he began to have dreams. At first he didn't understand what they were; he thought that what he dreamed was real.

Kaspar was gradually introduced to normal food. He finally ate meat. With his new diet and the pleasant family atmosphere, he grew rapidly. He learned to play chess and to help in the garden.

His senses of sight, smell, and hearing were all very sensitive. He could tell different kinds of fruit trees at a distance by the smell of their leaves. He said he felt a force coming from a magnet when it was near him. He could tell the north pole of a magnet from the south pole by the different feelings they gave him. But he could not do this for long, since it made him feel sick.

He was able to "feel" metals and to tell one metal from another without touching them. He said that a kind of chill went up his arm—different distances depending on the type of metal involved. He lost this sensitivity several months after he came to Nuremberg.

One morning Daumer's sister noticed drops of blood on the stairs leading to Kaspar's room. She went to his room to see if he had a nosebleed. He was not in his room, but there were bloody footprints there.

Daumer's mother found more blood spots, at the entrance to the cellar. Kaspar was found in the cellar, looking as if he were dead, with his face covered with blood. He was brought upstairs, where he showed he was alive by groaning, "Man, man."

He had been stabbed in the forehead. He stayed in bed for many days. Part of the time he was delirious, crying out, "Man, I love you too—don't kill! Why the man kill? I have done you nothing. Don't kill me! I will yet beg that you may not be locked up. Never have let me out of my prison, you would even kill me! You should first have killed me, before I understood what it is to live. You must say why you locked me up."

When he recovered, Kaspar said that he had been hit by a man whose head was covered in black. The man may have tried to stab him in the throat; Kaspar ducked and took the blow on the head. The would-be murderer saw him fall, saw a lot of blood, and thought he had succeeded.

This murder attempt took place in 1829. After Kaspar got well, an English lord, the Earl of Stanhope, became his guardian. The earl planned to take him to England, where he would be safe from further attempts on his life. Until that time, he would live in the town of Ansbach.

In Ansbach, in December of 1833, a second attempt was made on Kaspar's life. A man who apparently was a stranger talked to him in the park. He told Kaspar that he had a letter for him from his "mother." (His "mother" was Daumer's mother, who had treated him so well in Nuremberg.)

The stranger handed Kaspar a lady's handbag, saying the note was in it. While Kaspar was looking through the handbag for the note, the stranger stabbed him in the chest with a dagger. The point of the knife went into his heart.

The stranger ran away. Kaspar walked home, where he was put to bed. He died three days later.

The police found the handbag in the park. This note was in it:

Hauser can tell you exactly
How I look and who I am.
If Hauser will not take this trouble
Then I myself will say
I come — — — — —
I come from — — — —
Of the Bavarian border — — —
At the river — — —
And I will even tell you my name
                              M. L. O.

The meaning of the mysterious note has never been explained. Nor was the murderer ever caught.

Many people have been fascinated by this case and have written about it. Why would anyone keep a child locked up like that, and then let him go? Was the person criminally insane? Or is there some other explanation?

One theory sounds like the story of *The Man in the Iron Mask*, in which a twin, the rightful heir to a kingdom, is kept in a cell and forced to wear an iron mask to hide his identity. According to this theory, Kaspar was the heir to the throne of the Grand Duchy of Baden, a small independent state on the border between France and Germany. A crown prince was born to the royal family. He was thought to have died when he was only two weeks old. But there is evidence he was stolen. Another baby was substituted for him and then poisoned. The real royal baby was raised for three or four years by a nurse. After that, he was kept in a prison.

If Kaspar's mother did not have a son to succeed to the throne, the throne would go to another branch of the family. The heir in that branch was fairly old; if he didn't marry and have children before he died, then yet another branch of the family would get the throne. It was this last branch that went to such great efforts to steal Kaspar, kill his three brothers (it was claimed), and then keep Kaspar as insurance that the successor to the throne would not marry, because he knew that tucked away in a dungeon somewhere was this boy who would invalidate his claim to the throne.

When this man was about sixty-five and unlikely to have children, there was no longer any reason to keep Kaspar imprisoned. He was released. His keepers assumed he would disappear, since he would seem to be nothing but a feeble-minded peasant. But, instead, he was found by sympathetic people, adopted by the town of Nuremberg, and became widely known throughout Europe.

When the plotters in Baden heard he was writing his

memoirs, they would have been afraid that he had found out who he was. He might claim his rightful heritage. Therefore he had to die before their claim was disputed. And die he did.

This explanation may be true, but it has never been proven.

It is interesting that Kaspar did not have bad feelings about "the man with whom he had always been." When someone suggested he had been badly treated, Kaspar would say that he did not think so. It was his new life in the world that was hard. Now that he was among people, he saw how ignorant he was and how much he had to learn. So many things were beyond his understanding that they made his head ache.

When he had been in his cage, there had been no problems like this. He had been treated fairly well, he thought.

Once Kaspar thought that perhaps his jailer deserved punishment. This was when for the first time he saw the sky at night, full of stars. He was amazed and delighted at the sight of these lights in the sky. In Feuerbach's words: "'That,' he exclaimed, 'is, indeed, the most beautiful sight that I have ever yet seen in the world. But who has placed all these numerous candles there? Who lights them? Who puts them out?' When he was told that, like the sun, they always continue to give light, he asked again: who placed them there above, that they always continue to give light? At length, standing motionless, with his head bowed down, and his eyes staring, he fell into a train of deep and serious meditation. When he again recovered his recollection, his transport had been succeeded by deep sadness. He sank trembling upon a chair and asked why that wicked man had kept him always locked up and had never shown him any of these beautiful things. He, Kaspar, had never done any harm. He then broke into a fit of crying, which lasted for a long time, and which could with difficulty be soothed; and said that 'the man with whom he had always been' may now also be locked up for a few days, that he may learn to know how hard it is to be treated so."

To win a throne, an innocent boy may have been kept in a state worse than that of a wild animal. Certainly this was a grave crime. As Judge von Feuerbach concluded, it was "a crime committed against the life of the soul."

The most recent depiction of Kaspar Hauser is a German movie called *Every Man for Himself and God Against All* (it is also called *The Mystery of Kaspar Hauser*). The film follows the facts as presented by Feuerbach and others, with no attempt to solve the mystery. Like Truffaut's film about Victor of Aveyron, it is a study of the process of learning to adjust to life with other people, and of the growth of a mind confronted by new and puzzling things.

CHAPTER SIX

Indian Wolf Children

IN INDIA, where dense jungle sometimes begins at the edge of a village, there are many stories of children growing up in the wild and sometimes being brought up by wolves or other animals. One source of these stories is a pamphlet by Major General Sir William H. Sleeman. It was published in 1852.

It seems to be true that children have, from time to time, survived on their own in the jungle—by eating herbs, bark, or even small animals and carrion (dead animal flesh). But in a number of cases, the claim is made that the children survived because wild animals adopted them.

None of these cases of adoption has been proved conclusively. Some of them have been proved to be fraudulent. You must judge for yourself which parts of the following accounts are likely to be true. A lot of time has passed since the events described were supposed to have happened. It is too late for them to be investigated and proved either true or false. One famous case will be described in greater detail in the next two chapters.

In one case, an English soldier was riding next to a river when he saw a she-wolf, her three cubs, and a human child come out of a den in the river bank. The mother wolf seemed to care for the human child as much as for the cubs. The soldier tried to cut the boy off from the wolves, but his horse could not keep up with them on the uneven ground over which he chased them.

He got help from a nearby village. They dug the wolf family out of their den. The animals and boy made a break for it. The men caught the boy and tied him up in the village.

The boy was afraid of adults. But when a child came near, he would rush at it and try to bite. He would eat raw meat, but not cooked meat.

The soldier left the boy in the care of the Rajah of Hasunpoor. His parents turned up and recognized him as their child. When they found out how stupid he was, they decided to leave him where he was.

The boy refused to wear clothes. He was never seen to laugh or smile. He didn't talk. He would sometimes walk on all fours, and at other times on two legs. He was nine or ten years old when he was found. He died in 1850, three years later.

In 1843 an Indian woman took her three-year-old son with her when she went to work in the fields. He had recently burned his knee. While his mother worked, the boy sat on the grass, watching her.

Suddenly a wolf rushed from the bushes, grabbed the boy in its mouth, and carried him off. No one was able to stop the wolf.

Six years later, two men sitting by a river were astonished to see three wolf cubs and a boy come to the river to drink. The men chased the animals and boy back to their den. They caught the boy when he was halfway into the den. He resisted fiercely, biting when he could.

For the next twenty days the men kept him, feeding him raw meat. When they could not afford to feed him any longer, they set him loose in a village marketplace. They hoped that his human parents would recognize him and claim him. Until he was recognized, the boy would depend on the charity of the people of the village.

In time, the boy's mother heard about him. The burn mark and a birthmark convinced her that this was her child.

After the boy was home, he did not learn to talk. He followed his mother around only for the food she gave him. Since he did not improve and he showed no affection for her, she decided that she didn't care much for him either. After keeping him for two months, she turned him out to live on the charity of her village. People fed him during the day, and he spent his nights in the jungle.

The Rajah of Hasunpoor Bundooa described a twelve-year-old boy who wandered into town in 1843. He had "evidently been brought up by wolves." The boy was said to have short dark hairs all over his body. They fell out after he began eating meat that had been salted.

Although he could walk in a normal fashion, he was unable to talk. He made sounds but did not speak words. He was recognized by his parents. They took him away, and he was never heard of again.

One wonders why people were sure he had been raised by wolves. There was no claim that he had even been seen with wolves. The part about the body hair is probably not true. He must have looked hairy because he was very dirty after living in the jungle. Rather than being raised by wolves, the boy may have been a mentally retarded child who had wandered away from home and gotten lost.

In the village of Ghutkoree, a shepherd saw a boy trotting along on all fours beside a wolf. He ran after the boy. The boy was very fast, but the shepherd caught him.

The shepherd kept the boy with him and fed him. Despite the shepherd's efforts, the boy would not associate with people nor would he speak. Eventually, the boy ran off into the jungle and was not heard of again.

Another of the stories reported to General Sleeman was of a soldier near Sultanpoor who was accompanied by a boy of nine or ten. He claimed he had rescued the boy from wolves. The boy ate everything given to him, including bread. Before eating, he would smell his food very carefully. He walked on two legs, but calluses on his knees and elbows showed that he had been used to moving on all fours.

He did not talk, but he did not seem to mind wearing clothes. A man appeared who claimed to be the boy's father. He said the boy had been taken away by wolves when he was six years old.

Two soldiers saw a ten-year-old boy drinking at a stream with two wolf cubs. They caught the boy and brought him to Rajah Hurdut Sing of Bondee. He was tied up in a shed and given raw meat to eat.

The boy tried to escape a few times. After a while, the Rajah let him go, since he was so much trouble to take care of. Other people would keep him for a while. But they would also grow tired of him and let him go.

He smelled very bad and had filthy habits. Eventually he was taught to walk on two feet.

One night the boy was seen playing with two wolves.

The next night there were three wolves. It was thought that these were the wolves he had shared a den with and had been rescued from.

Finally, the boy ran away and was not found again. Two months after his escape, a woman asked if the boy had had scars of a certain kind on his chest and forehead. She was sure that the boy was her son who had

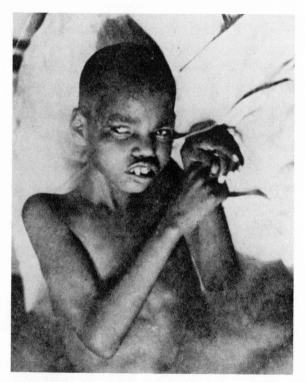

Indian child believed to have been brought up by wolves. (*N. Y. Public Library Picture Collection*)

been taken from her by a wolf five years before. But the boy was not found again.

General Sleeman was willing to believe in the truth of these cases. He had an interesting explanation of why no wolf boys grew up to be wolf men. He believed they were killed by other wolves or by tigers that came across the children eating at the tigers' kill.

There are many other Indian cases. In 1874 an English doctor described a case that was clearly a fake. The boy was fourteen and supposedly unable to speak. But within ten days he had not only learned to talk, but to argue as well. He was able to describe what it was like to live in a wolf's den.

When he went on all fours to show how he had traveled with the wolves, he did such a poor job of it that the doctor said, "The wolves would have had a bad dinner on the day this gentleman joined in their wild sports."

It seemed fairly certain that this fraud was simply a money-making scheme.

In 1920 it was claimed that a child had been captured and raised for a short time by a leopard. The child's father said that he could not do his work because he had to take care of his wild son; if he didn't watch the boy, he would run away into the jungle.

The European who had wanted the man to work for him went to see what this boy was like. He was about seven years old. When he saw the man, he ran away on all fours and hid between his father's legs. His body was covered with small white scars that were probably healed scratches. He was almost completely blind from cataracts or some similar condition.

The observer presented the story without deciding himself whether it was true or not. Five years before, two leopard cubs had been killed near the village. The mother leopard had tracked the killers to the village.

Meanwhile, the boy's mother had taken him to the fields. She put him down on a cloth while she worked. When she heard the baby cry, she saw a leopard carrying him away. The entire village chased after the leopard. When darkness fell, they were unable to follow it any longer. They decided that the leopard would have eaten the child by morning.

Three years later, a leopard was killed near the village. Two cubs and the boy were found. The boy had heavy calluses on his hands and knees, from walking on all fours. He fought and bit everyone he could get hold of. In time, he learned to get along with the villagers, identifying them by smell. The blindness had been only partial when he was captured, and did not seem to have anything to do with his life with the leopard.

He would eat raw meat, and he also learned to eat the regular diet of the village. If a chicken came close to him, he would grab it, kill it, rip the feathers off, and eat it on the spot.

Many cases similar to these have been reported. The evidence given to prove that the children were raised by wolves is usually circumstantial—the behavior of the children or the fact that they cannot walk upright or that they have been found in wolf dens. But there are many cases of children who have never seen a wolf, yet act in similar ways because of mental disturbance. It is quite possible for a child to take shelter in a wolf den when there are no wolves in residence.

With so many stories from India of children being raised by wolves, it is not surprising that a writer would take this theme and make up stories of his own about a human child raised by wolves. The Mowgli stories in Rudyard Kipling's *Jungle Books* are the best-known examples.

A little boy, just big enough to walk, doesn't know it, but he is being hunted by Shere Khan, a man-eating tiger. Just in time, he wanders into a wolf den—hungry, naked, alone, but unafraid. The mother wolf decides to raise him with her cubs. She gives him the name Mowgli —the frog.

The tiger comes to claim the boy as his lawful prey. The wolves, who know the tiger is too big to get into their den, send Shere Khan on his way. The mother wolf vows that when the boy is grown, it is the man-child that will be the hunter, and Shere Khan will be the hunted.

Mowgli is accepted into the pack. He is taught the ways of the jungle by a bear and a panther.

Shere Khan's hatred of the boy grows. Through flattery and sharing his kill, the tiger is able to turn some of the younger wolves of the pack against the man-child. At a jungle council they decide to kill Mowgli.

But Mowgli is ready for them. From a nearby village he has stolen a clay pot full of the red flower. The red flower is fire. He lights a torch in this pot of fire. He drives back Shere Khan.

Now that he has been rejected by the pack, he decides to leave the jungle and return to the world of men. As he leaves, he vows that one day he will return to lay the skin of Shere Khan on the council rock.

That is the first of the Mowgli stories. There are other stories about Mowgli and his brothers, the wolves, and other animals—some enemies and some friends. He has dealings with the world of men and finds his own human mother and saves her life. Unlike the wolf children in supposedly factual accounts, Mowgli learns not only the animals' languages but also human speech. And he walks upright, not on all fours.

In the next chapters we will consider the best-known case of Indian wolf-children, Amala and Kamala of Midnapore.

CHAPTER SEVEN

Amala and Kamala—The Girls from the Wolf Den

EVERY YEAR the missionary traveled into the Indian jungle in search of tribal people to convert. The jungle was full of wild animals, including jackals, tigers, and wolves. When the missionary and his men stopped for the night, they posted armed guards and set a circle of fires around their camp. Often they saw the light of the fires reflected in the eyes of animals prowling in the outer darkness.

On one of these trips, in 1920, the missionary came to a village where the people were worried about a manush-bagha, or man-ghost. A manush-bagha has arms and legs like a man, but the head of a ghost. The villagers asked the missionary to drive the creature away. He agreed to do this. The missionary—the Reverend

J. A. L. Singh—described the following events in a book he published many years later, based on journals he kept.

Rev. Singh—who was a native Indian himself—was taken to where the man-ghost had been seen. It was a wolf den in an old white-ant mound. These mounds are common in tropical countries. They can be as high as a two-story building.

Singh had a platform built. From it the men could observe the mound in safety when the man-ghost came out at dusk. If necessary, they could try to shoot it with their rifles.

At dusk a full-grown wolf came out of an opening in the ant mound. Then another full-grown wolf came out, followed by a third. Then two wolf cubs came out into the dim evening light. So far, nothing unusual.

Then in Singh's own words, "Close after the cubs came the ghost—a hideous-looking being—hand, foot, and body like a human being; but the head was a big ball of something covering the shoulders and the upper portion of the bust, leaving only a sharp contour of the face visible, and it was human. Close at its heels there came another awful creature exactly like the first, but smaller in size. Their eyes were bright and piercing, unlike human eyes."

Nevertheless, Singh was sure these two creatures were human. Both of them looked around cautiously before coming out of the ant mound. They walked on all fours.

The other men on the platform did not recognize the creatures as humans. As a result, they were taking aim with their rifles. The dim light made it difficult to take aim, or they would have fired immediately.

Singh stopped them in time. After taking a good look through binoculars, all but one man agreed that the monsters were human children. One man, however, was still certain they were ghosts.

The next day, the wolves and children were seen again. Singh decided to capture the children. He tried to get the local villagers to help him dig into the ant mound. But Chuna, the man from the platform who believed they were ghosts, had told the villagers that they were indeed ghosts. The villagers would not help Singh. They believed that the ghosts, if disturbed, would come back to their village and kill them all.

Singh went to another village. The people had never heard of the ghosts. He hired a crew to cut a door-sized opening in the ant mound.

Shortly after the men began to dig, two wolves escaped from the mound and ran for their lives. But the third wolf tried to chase the diggers away. She howled, gnashed her teeth, and showed every sign that she would defend the mound to her death. Rather than be attacked by this fierce wolf, who was probably the mother of the cubs, the workmen killed her with their bows and arrows. Singh later decided that the wolf must have originally brought the children to her den as food for her cubs. Then her maternal feelings must have taken over, causing her to nurture them instead.

When the workmen dug into the mound, they found

an inner room. The two wolf cubs and the two ghosts were all huddled together in the corner.

To separate them, Singh threw a piece of cloth over them. He pulled one of the cubs apart from the group. He then tied the cloth into a kind of bag with the cub inside. Then he used other pieces of cloth to separate the others.

The job was done. He paid off the workers and gave them the wolf cubs to sell as pets.

Now that the children had been captured, Singh felt free to go on with his regular missionary work. He found someone to take care of the children for the few days he would be away. It was Chuna, the only one of the original party who would not believe that the ghosts were really human. He turned out to be an unfortunate choice for a babysitter.

The two bedraggled little girls were put in a corral in Chuna's yard. A pot of rice and a pot of water were put in the corral so they could eat and drink. Chuna agreed to look after them.

As soon as Singh left, Chuna packed up his family and fled to parts unknown. He wasn't going to have anything to do with the ghosts. The rest of the village was as frightened as he had been. They too left to get away from the fierce man-ghosts.

For five days the girls were left in the corral without care. They had probably been in a state of shock when they were penned up because of the violence of their

Amala and Kamala—The Girls from the Wolf Den

Kamala receiving food.

capture. Now, after days of neglect, it was a miracle that they were not dead of hunger, thirst, and fright.

When he returned, Singh was alarmed to see how

terrible their condition had become. He was unable to get them to eat. Finally, he found that they would suck on a handkerchief moistened with milk. They recovered some of their strength.

After a few days they were somewhat stronger. But this was not the end of their ordeal. They were taken by ox cart over seventy-five miles of rough roads to the Rev. Singh's orphanage in Midnapore. With frequent stops for rest, the trip took eight days.

The only person to whom Rev. Singh dared to tell the story of the girls' capture was his wife. He would not even have a doctor come to treat them. He was afraid that if the story were generally known, the interest of the public and the newspapers would bring crowds to the orphanage that would interfere with his work.

The older girl, who was about eight years old, was given the name Kamala. The younger—about a year and a half old—was named Amala.

They were fed milk and vegetables. Although they were very fond of raw meat, Singh was afraid that if he gave it to them, it would make them fierce, and they were already wild enough. They did not eat with their hands; instead, they brought their mouths to the food— as dogs and wolves do. On one occasion Kamala ate *with* a dog, sharing its plate of food and snarling at anyone who tried to interfere. The dog didn't seem to mind.

If Kamala found any small dead animal on the orphanage grounds, she quickly ate it. She was very skillful in stripping the feathers off dead birds.

Amala and Kamala—The Girls from the Wolf Den

The girls preferred the company of animals to that of people. They had been used to it; more important, they probably thought of themselves as animals. Somehow the animals at the orphanage sensed that these girls were different, and they accepted them as animals.

The only sound either girl made at first was a hoarse cry that ended in "a thrilling shrill wailing." It would have been a call they learned from the wolves. They regularly used it during the night.

Another trait they had in common with animals, according to Singh, was the way their eyes glared in the dark, seeming to give off a soft blue light. This kind of glare is very rare in humans—if, in fact, it exists at all— and is due to reflection of light. The girls could also see better at night than during the day. This seems likely since they were leading the nocturnal life of wolves.

Amala and Kamala, like other wild children, had a good sense of smell. They would smell everything carefully before eating. They were sensitive to noise and to touch.

They walked on all fours. When traveling slowly, they went on their hands and knees. To go faster, they would get up on hands and feet.

They did not like the daylight. During the day they would stay in the darkest corner of their room. When dusk came, they would become restless and wish to go out. They would roam about in the darkness. Neither of them ever laughed. For three years after she was captured, Kamala was never known to laugh or smile.

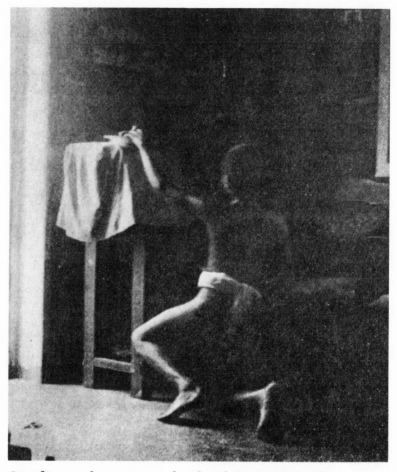

Standing on knees to reach a bowl containing milk.

A little more than eleven months after their capture, both girls fell sick. They appeared to be in a coma for about five days. They suffered from dysentery, worms, and chills and fever.

Amala and Kamala—The Girls from the Wolf Den

Because of the serious nature of their illness, Rev. Singh had felt obliged to get a doctor to see the girls. The doctor sensed that these girls were something out of the ordinary. Singh had hoped to keep their origin a secret. Then if they were able to learn the ways of normal humans, they would have some hope of leading regular lives—they would not be saddled with the name "wolf girls" by a curious public.

But this illness had clearly endangered their lives. The doctor insisted on being told their history, so he could treat them properly.

Rev. Singh and his wife decided they had very little choice. The girls seemed near death. If revealing their secret gave them some chance for life, it would be worthwhile. They told the doctor all they knew about the girls.

The doctor, unfortunately, could not keep his mouth shut. "I requested the doctor very earnestly not to divulge the secret," Singh wrote. "But unfortunately this request only added impetus to his desire for publication. The next day all the families in the town, wherever he went, knew all about the wolf-children in our orphanage at Midnapore."

Despite prayers and medical attention, Amala died. On that day Kamala shed the first tears she had been known to let fall. They were tears without a frown or other expression of grief.

With her companion gone, Kamala became more attentive to the animals around the orphanage, especially the baby goats. As time went by, she took on characteristics that were more and more appropriate to a human child, though of a child of retarded mental development.

From a creature with a fondness for raw meat so great that she would drive vultures away from the carrion they were feeding on, she became a little girl who would be picky about the amount of salt on her cooked meat. After a while the dogs barked at her as they did at other people. She, in turn, became afraid of them. And she became afraid of the dark.

During the eight years following Amala's death, Kamala made some progress as a result of the Singhs' attention and training, and from the contact she had with the other children at the orphanage. The first stage, begun before Amala's death, involved developing the girls' senses. (A similar process was carried out by Itard with Victor.)

Mrs. Singh would massage the girls for an hour each day. They hated it at first, but later they enjoyed the contact and were soothed by it. Singh writes that "the love expressed in tone and action was gradually understood." Mrs. Singh would play with them and caress them. Kamala eventually was very affectionate toward Mrs. Singh and took an interest in the other children.

By imitating the other children, Kamala learned to say several words for objects found around the orphanage. She also learned to say people's names. She did not, however, really speak.

Kamala's way of eating was to lap up food.

Getting Kamala to stand and walk on her feet—not on all fours—was a long and difficult process. She was forced to reach higher and higher for her food. First she

81

had to learn to move on her knees (without the support of her hands), then to lift herself onto her feet. Finally —in response to the task of reaching for her food—Kamala learned to walk for short times in the normal human fashion.

In 1929, Kamala became sick and died. Singh said that at the time of her death she had been "reclaimed from the ferocious temper, wild habits, and the completely different being of an animal." He estimated her age to be sixteen.

Were Amala and Kamala genuine cases of children raised by animals? According to Singh, they were. In the next chapter we will look at the work of a scientist who set out to find out just how true Singh's story was.

CHAPTER EIGHT

Amala and Kamala— Epilogue: The Missing Village

TWENTY-TWO YEARS after Kamala's death, an American professor of sociology went to India to do some detective work. He had read Rev. Singh's report and was interested in the story of the two wolf girls.

It seemed to the professor, William F. Ogburn, that this might be the last chance science would have to study children raised by animals. Since there were fewer and fewer wild places left in the world, he didn't think it likely that a similar case would happen again. (The gazelle boy was a later case, but there was no scientific study or verification of the facts.) Ogburn wanted to study the effect of rearing by animals on human personality development.

Even though the two girls, as well as the Rev. and Mrs.

Singh and other important sources, were now dead, Ogburn hoped that he would be able to find other people who had known Kamala. Men and women who had spent part of their childhood at the orphanage would have grown up with Kamala as a playmate. He might learn many important things that were never mentioned in Singh's diary.

But first he had to determine whether the girls had really been reared by wolves. If they were not reared by wolves, the rest of the study would be pointless. If Singh's story of the rescue from the wolf den was untrue, then there would be good reason to doubt the truth of the rest of his report. It could not, therefore, be used as the basis of scientific study. So Ogburn decided to turn detective and search out the truth.

The investigation was conducted by Ogburn and a team of Indian scientists. At first Ogburn hired a detective agency in Calcutta to do some of the preliminary work. The agency could not locate the village of Godamuri where the capture was supposed to have taken place, nor could they find any people who had been children at the orphanage while Kamala was there.

The only way for Ogburn to get results seemed to be to do the job himself and through his colleagues. They visited Rev. Singh's daughter at the orphanage in Midnapore. There had been an earlier visit; Singh's daughter had told the story of the capture pretty much as it was written in the diary. But on this second occasion, she remembered that a visiting minister had seen Kamala

Kamala in a corner.

eating chicken entrails and suggested that she ought to be called wolf-girl. Singh's daughter also said that Kamala had more than the normal amount of body hair.

During this stage of the investigation, an old lawyer had been visited. He confirmed that the girls had lived at the orphanage during the period claimed and that they had been supposedly rescued from a tiger's den.

A tiger's den? Until now it was a wolf's den they had been rescued from. Throughout the investigation there were some people who would say the girls had been rescued from a wolf's den; others would speak of a tiger's den. This is less of a problem than it may seem at first. In the Bengali language the word *bagh* is used for both tigers and wolves; it is more a problem of translation than anything else. The lawyer said that Kamala did *not* have excessive body hair.

During the second visit to Singh's daughter, the investigators found that she had heard stories of wolf children from her grandmother—before Amala and Kamala had been captured—and that her father had written about wolf children before the two girls came on the scene. She did not know where the village of Godamuri, near the scene of the capture, was.

In Midnapore they found one woman who had lived at the orphanage and remembered Kamala. She, like the lawyer, said that Kamala did not have a hairy body. She also claimed that Singh did not capture the girls. She said it was her uncle who had found them in the forest. There was much in the book that was not true, she said, put in to make it a good story. A local minister's wife who was present during this interview agreed with her that there was much in the book that was not true.

The woman's uncle was dead. But other sources made it seem more likely that the girls had been captured by someone other than Singh. For example, there was a newspaper account—printed about a year after the reported capture of the girls and shortly after Amala's death—which maintained that the girls were taken from a tiger's den by local people and brought to Rev. Singh for him to take care of.

Amala and Kamala—Epilogue: The Missing Village

This newspaper story was very likely based on information supplied by Singh. Yet it does not mention the place of capture, the termite mound, or any of the people in Singh's diary account.

In their prolonged search for the site of the capture, Ogburn and his associates interviewed many people and corresponded with a number of government officials concerning the probable location of the village. Most of the stories were in agreement as to the general location. But when it was visited by jeep, none of the local elders had ever heard anything about the incident.

Where was the village? Whether the girls came from a wolf den or not, they had to come from some place. Singh may have disguised the name or the location for some reason of his own.

What about the truth of the capture itself? Only Singh's daughter—and, later, his son—maintained that he captured the girls from a wolf den. Yet neither of them was present at the event; they simply had read the account in their father's book. No one could be found who had been present at the capture.

This negative evidence does not prove that Amala and Kamala were *not* reared in a wolf den. But the absence of positive evidence makes it impossible to be certain that they were.

No one has presented evidence that Rev. Singh was deliberately trying to mislead people about Amala and Kamala. But the research by Ogburn and his associates suggests that Singh may have become confused or mis-

Kamala and Amala asleep.

led himself in his memory of the children's capture—perhaps under the influence of the existing folklore about wolf children or, as some of the people interviewed suggested, to attract attention and funds for his orphanage, or to write a more interesting book.

The story of Amala and Kamala provides one more example of the difficulty of training a child whose formative years were spent in isolation from human adults. At the same time, the doubts raised by Ogburn remove from certainty what had seemed to be the most likely modern case of animals rearing human children.

CHAPTER NINE

The Wolf Boy of Agra

In addition to following Amala and Kamala's trail, William Ogburn studied another wolf-child case. He read the following information in Indian newspapers.

Soldiers on a hunting trip rode up to a stream. They saw that some wolves had also come to the stream to drink. The men chased the animals. Two of them were full-grown wolves; the third appeared to be a cub. Before they could run the animals down and shoot them, they saw that the cub was really a human child.

They separated the child from the running wolves and captured him. In town, the Jatav family recognized the boy as their own child who had been taken from them by wolves four and a half years before.

Ogburn was already in India. He went to Agra, the

nearest city, and to some of the villages mentioned in the newspapers. He spoke with the family who had claimed the wolf boy as their own.

He found that the family had indeed lost a child when he was eighteen months old. The mother and boy had been sleeping outside their house. The mother woke and found that her baby was gone. Since she saw a wolf running away, she assumed that the wolf had the child in its jaws and was taking it away.

It was apparently not unusual for children to be stolen by animals in this way. The same week as Ogburn's visit, he read in the newspapers of a child being stolen by a hyena. He also learned that the child of a colleague's brother had been stolen by a wolf; the wolf had been killed and the child was recovered unharmed.

It is almost certain that in these cases the children were stolen by the animals for food. But a retriever can carry a wounded bird in its mouth so firmly and carefully that it will neither escape nor be injured further. In the same way, wild animals are able to carry children without harming them, even though they intend to eat them later.

Ogburn's impression of the child was that he was not at all like wolf children that he had read about, especially Amala and Kamala, who were very shy of people. Parasram, as the boy was called, was not at all afraid of strangers. Nor did he at any time crawl around on all fours. "My first impression of Parasram," Ogburn wrote, "was that of an exhibitionistic, spoiled child whose parents have had him do his stunt before visitors who are supposed to admire him." The boy was not interested in people in any way. He seemed to think of people as objects. He hardly spoke, knowing only a few words.

How had the parents recognized the child as their own after so many years? The boy's father pointed to a small scar on the top of the boy's head. Their baby had had a boil there, which had burst and left a scar. Likewise, there was a scar on his neck, where their baby had had another boil.

At this point, the story of the wolf boy may begin to seem doubtful. One can't be sure that a wolf took the child. His mother noticed that the child was missing; when she looked up, she saw a wolf. This does not mean that the wolf took the child. It might have simply been in the area, and there may have been some other reason for the child's disappearance.

The way the child acted also raised doubts for Ogburn. He did not crawl around like other wolf children. He was quite active during the day, while other wolf children tend to be quiet during the day.

Ogburn questioned the parents further. How did they get their child back? They said he had been given to them by a man name Indraj Sharma.

Ogburn's next step was to find Sharma. He was living in a village about twenty-four miles away. He had been in the army for ten years, but now ran a bicycle shop. He did not speak English, but through the use of an interpreter, many interesting things were learned.

It turned out that the boy had been found by Sharma, not by soldiers. Sharma had been alone when he found him, and there were no animals of any kind near the boy when he was found. The child had lived with Sharma's family for four months without ever being linked to wolves. It was not until the boy's parents claimed him that the wolf story was circulated in the press.

Could the parents have been wrong about this boy? Would they have wanted to adopt a child who was theirs only by very flimsy evidence? They had two daughters but no son, their only son being the one who disappeared —or was taken by the wolf. Like many people in India, they very much wanted to have a son, perhaps even to claim this strange boy as their own on the basis of skimpy evidence. Since the boy could not talk, he was not in any position to contradict them.

The boy was an unusual child, although there was no real evidence to suggest that his oddities were due to being raised by wolves. Perhaps he was retarded or had an undiagnosed glandular condition. A lucky series of accidents had found a home for this child who may well have lived on his own in the wild, but almost certainly was not a genuine wolf boy.

Many details of his story—including the discovery by soldiers—may remind you of other stories told about Indian wolf children. The facts in the case seem to have been embroidered with details from earlier tales. This is how legends grow.

CHAPTER TEN

Tarzan and Other Apemen

Tarzan of the apes is probably the best-known wild child of all time. He is, of course, the fictional creation of Edgar Rice Burroughs.

The name Tarzan means "white-skin" in ape language and was given to him by Kala, the ape who adopted him. His real parents, in the book *Tarzan of the Apes*, are Lord and Lady Greystoke of England. Through a series of unusual circumstances, the Greystokes are stranded on the west coast of Africa, where their son is born. His mother nurses him for a year and then dies.

How can the father keep this child alive by himself? He despairs and sits at the table of his cabin with his head in his hands. At this point, three bull apes enter the cabin and kill Lord Greystoke. A she-ape, Kala, follows them and finds the baby crying in his cradle.

Kala's own baby has just been killed in a fall from its mother's back while she was swinging through the trees. Her maternal instincts prompt her to take the living human baby and put her dead baby in its place in the cradle. She puts Tarzan to her breast and nurses him.

It is almost ten years before Tarzan realizes he is not an ape. His discovery fills him with shame. He tries to make himself look more like an ape by coating himself with dark clay, but it is so uncomfortable and ineffective that he decides to put up with the shame instead.

The growing boy has many exciting adventures. He teaches himself to swin, how to use the knife he has found in the cabin, and, most amazingly, he teaches himself to read. He does this with the aid of some children's books he finds in the cabin.

In time, Tarzan meets other Europeans. They have been put ashore as the result of a mutiny; later they are rescued by a French warship. One of the people who falls victim to the mutineers is Jane Porter.

Although Tarzan has taught himself to read and write English, he has never learned to speak it. His only spoken language is "apish." After prolonged contact with the Europeans, a French naval officer teaches him to speak a human language, French.

Eventually Tarzan discovers that he is the son of Lord

Tarzan. From *Tarzan, the Ape Man.* (*MGM*)

Greystoke. He and Jane marry and establish a plantation in East Africa. There are many books that follow the career of Tarzan and films have been made also. These things have brought millions of people into contact with the notion of a child raised by animals.

The circumstances under which Tarzan is adopted by Kala are unusual and fictional in the number of lucky coincidences needed for the adoption to take place. But

95

they are similar to the circumstances claimed in "true" cases of adoption of human children by animals.

Kipling's stories in *The Jungle Books* about the wolf-boy Mowgli were one of Burroughs' inspirations for Tarzan. He also made use of a story that he read somewhere about a sailor shipwrecked on the coast of Africa who lived among apes for many years.

There are claims from time to time that real children have been brought up by apes or monkeys. In fact, a number of modern-day scientists have observed that chimpanzees and other apes seem to have an instinctive interest in other species of animals. For example, a troop of chimpanzees in Uganda included a monkey that seemed to have been adopted and raised by the troop. It is only natural, moreover, that the most human of animals would be associated with humans in the age-old mythology of animals adopting human children.

In 1976 a boy turned up in the African country of Burundi who had supposedly been brought up by monkeys. He was given the name of John—after John the Baptist, who had also lived in the wilderness.

This case was studied by two American professors. One of them was Harlan Lane, who has written a book about Victor of Aveyron. The professors found that the boy had never been in the wild and that there weren't even any monkeys in the part of the country that he was supposed to have come from.

The facts of the case were that John lost both his parents in the first year of his life. When he was about two, he suffered a very serious illness, which caused brain damage and mental retardation. He made noises like a monkey, which led people to conclude that he had been raised by monkeys.

In the course of being shifted from place to place, his records were lost. He had lived in three orphanages and one psychiatric ward. Without parents, without a name, without a normal mind, this ten year old became the subject of a made-up life history that had no relation to the facts.

To go back to the question of why there aren't more cases of children raised by apes or monkeys, it is useful to consider the story of Tarzan's adoptive mother, Kala. She had lost her own baby. It has been suggested that this is what would happen if an ape tried to adopt a human baby. She would pick it up and put it on her back when she took off through the trees. An ape baby would have the instincts and ability to cling to its mother's back by holding on to her fur. But a human baby would not, and would soon fall to the ground, dying as a result of the fall.

This is only a theory. It seems to make sense, but it is not known to be either true or false. It is easy to jump from thinking "this makes sense" to "this must be true" to "this is a fact." This process happens again and again

97

in stories like the one about John, the "monkey-boy," and in many of the wolf-child stories from India. It is a dangerous process—dangerous in the way we can end up confusing fact and fiction.

CHAPTER ELEVEN

Pecos Bill

THE STORY OF PECOS BILL is not the usual account of a child growing up in the wild. You don't have to wonder how much of the story may or may not be true, since the whole story is made up. Its purpose is to amuse.

Bill's story is a tall tale of the Wild West. He was born in east Texas. A normal Texas baby, he was weaned on corn whiskey and cut his teeth on a bowie knife.

When Bill's parents learned that a neighbor had moved within fifty miles of them, they decided that the area was getting too thickly settled. So they packed Bill and his seventeen brothers and sisters into the back of a covered wagon and headed west.

All went well until they were crossing the Pecos River. A bump caused Bill to tumble out of the wagon. By the time his parents got around to counting noses, they had gone too far to go back to hunt for Bill.

But Bill wasn't too bad off. He found, or was found by, a pack of coyotes. They brought him up on coyote milk and, when he was older, on wild fruits and berries and assorted coyote food.

He took to the life and grew up speaking coyote as his first language. In fact, he *was* a coyote as far as he knew. The coyotes were mighty proud of their human. He learned so well that he out-coyoted the coyotes.

He was a swift runner and able hunter of antelope and jackrabbits. He was a useful member of the pack when it came to pulling thorns and cactus spines out of the paws of brother coyotes. In the evening he could sit on his haunches and howl at the moon with the best of them.

One day he was out hunting for a deer to run off its feet or a bear to hug to death. Instead, he found one of the wildest and strangest creatures on earth, a Texas cowboy. Naturally, he didn't know what the creature was. The smell of this cowboy thing was a little strange to his sensitive coyote nose and, at the same time, a little bit familiar too. His nose remembered what his mind had forgotten.

After some weeks the cowboy learned enough coyote talk and Bill learned enough cowboy talk so the two of them could talk to each other. The cowboy thought this boy with the long red hair, all-over suntan, and muscles from chasing antelope was the strangest human he'd ever seen. Bill was trying to figure out what it was about the cowboy that seemed familiar.

When they were able to talk together, the cowboy asked Bill why he ran around naked and howled like a coyote.

Bill answered, "Because I *am* a coyote."

"You ain't no coyote. You're a human, just like me."

"I am not. I got fleas and I howl at the moon all night."

"That don't mean a thing. Texans have fleas, and most of them howl a lot. If you're a coyote, where's your tail?"

Bill looked at himself. No tail. He hadn't thought of that. "Well, there you go. It looks like I'm a human. Show me some more humans and I'll join up."

That is how his fabulous career as a cowboy began. He invented any number of cowboy devices—like the six-shooter—and useful activities like roping and train-robbing. All this sounds pretty simple and reasonable, of course, but how did Bill know that his name was Bill and that he fell out of a wagon near the Pecos River?

Well, it turned out that the cowboy who taught Bill to talk had a star tattoo on his arm. Bill noticed that he had one on his own arm in the same place. When he pointed this out, the cowboy explained that his mother had had a star tattooed on his arm and on the arms of all his brothers and sisters so they would never forget that they came from Texas.

If Bill had the same star tattoo, that meant he was his

long-lost brother Bill who had fallen out of the wagon when his family was moving west. Was it any wonder that the cowboy smelled familiar?

As for the many other things that made him a well-known figure in the West—things that he did after he stopped being a coyote—consult a book of folklore. If you're lucky enough to live in the West, ask some of the old hands about Pecos Bill.

CHAPTER TWELVE

The Wolf Girl of Devil's River

DEVIL'S RIVER is located about 150 miles west of San Antonio, Texas. It is about 20 miles east of the Pecos River.

In May 1835, according to the story, a man named John Dent came to a ranch to get help for his wife. They were camped on Devil's River, and she was about to give birth. Dent was killed in a freak electrical storm before he could return to his wife Mollie with the rancher and the rancher's wife.

When the rancher and his wife got to the campsite, they found that Mollie Dent had died giving birth. But the child couldn't be found. From tracks nearby, the rancher suspected that wolves had eaten the baby.

Ten years later, a boy claimed he saw a naked girl

among a pack of wolves that were attacking a herd of goats. About a year after that, a woman claimed she saw a naked girl and two wolves eating a freshly killed goat. When the woman surprised them, the wolves and the girl ran away together. The girl at first ran on all fours and then got up and ran on two feet.

People wondered if this was Mollie Dent's missing child. They knew how wolves picked up their cubs by the scruff of the neck and carried them without hurting them. Maybe the infant had been picked up in the same way and carried off to be brought up by a female wolf.

They decided to try to capture the girl. After a three-day search, they spotted her and cornered her. At first it seemed that the pack had abandoned her, but suddenly a large wolf leaped out at the men. They were able to shoot the attacking wolf before he injured or killed anyone.

The girl had been spitting and snarling at the men, but when the wolf was killed, she fainted. They tied her up and took her to the nearest ranch.

The men put her in a room with a board nailed across the only window. They untied her and offered her clothes, food, and water.

The girl just backed into a dark corner and stayed there until they left her and closed the door. When darkness fell, she began to make frightening noises that were a combination of a woman's screaming and a wolf's howling.

This would have been eerie enough to listen to, but there was more. The ranch was in the heart of an uninhabited wilderness. The men began to feel just how isolated they were when the strange calls of the wolf girl began to be answered by the howls of real wolves all around them. They had never heard so many wolves before. And the howls were getting closer.

After a while the deep-throated chorus of wolves stopped, as though they were waiting for something. Then the girl resumed her howling screams from inside the ranch house. A little while later, the wolf pack attacked the ranch's goats, milk cows, and horses.

This spurred the men into action. They went out after the wolves, yelling and shooting into the darkness as they charged them. They were able to drive them off. But when they returned to the ranch house, they discovered that during the confusion the wolf girl had managed to tear the board off the window and leap to freedom. When daylight came, there was no trace or track of the wolf girl.

For the next six years, not only was there no trace of the girl, but even wolves became scarce in the area. It was not until 1852 that a party of frontiersmen hunting for a new route to El Paso came upon a naked young woman nursing two wolf cubs. As soon as she saw the men, she grabbed up the cubs, one under each arm, and ran off like the wind.

She was never, as far as is known, seen again. But

according to ranchers, it became common to find wolves in the area that had a markedly human look about their faces.

It is only these last two paragraphs, one might think, that make the story of the wolf girl less than believable. How could a human give birth to wolf cubs?

Perhaps the story of the wolf girl is folklore that had its origin in some actual events, with later impossible additions. Or the story may have been influenced by wolf-child stories that were brought from Europe by early settlers. We will probably never know.

CHAPTER THIRTEEN

Raised by Martians

A HUMAN CHILD that grows up alone in the forest is unlikely to ever grow into a normal human adult. If it is possible for a human child to be raised by animals, as has been claimed, the child isn't likely to be any better off in adjusting to human society when he or she is rescued from the wild.

So far, we have looked only at children who were supposed to have grown up alone or with creatures of subhuman intelligence. But what if a child were raised by creatures of *super*human intelligence? Then he or she might grow up to be a superhuman adult, better than ordinary people.

Robert A. Heinlein wrote a novel entitled *Stranger in a Strange Land* about a man who was born in a spaceship and raised on Mars by Martians. Since his human parents were dead, he did not see another human until he was in his twenties.

His name was Valentine Michael Smith. His parents were both very intelligent people; his father was the commander of the expedition that brought them to Mars, and his mother was the spaceship's atomics engineer and electronics and power technician.

The Martians went through a five-stage life cycle. They started as eggs and hatched out into a nymph stage. The nymphs were "fat, furry spheres, full of bounce and mindless energy." Only about one out of nine nymphs survived to the next, or nestling, stage, from which they eventually metamorphosed into adult Martians. The adults were "huge, reminding the first humans to see them of ice boats under sail."

In the fullness of time, the adults would "discorporate" and become "Old Ones," which were essentially the souls of dead Martians. Although dead, they were frequently called on for advice and were really in control of the planet.

The "discorporation" of an adult was usually voluntary. After it had taken place, the surviving Martians ate the body of the discorporated adult so that they could cherish not only the memory of the departed, but his flavor as well. As a result, voluntary discorporations took place frequently during times of food shortage. Unusual stress could cause *involuntary* discorporation.

Since the only survivor of the Mars expedition was a baby, no one back on Earth knew what had happened. World War III delayed a relief expedition until twenty-five years had passed. The second expedition found Valentine Michael Smith and brought him back to Earth. Mike, as he was called, didn't want to go, but the Old Ones told him that he must.

On Earth he was at first in constant danger of discorporating. He took a while to get used to gravity that was two and a half times what he was used to on Mars. It took him a long time to get used to the high emotional content of human existence. It was months before he felt that he too was human—when he laughed for the first time.

There was much that he brought with him to Earth in the form of his Martian upbringing. At first he was a skinny kid with a babyface and very old-looking eyes. Later he changed his looks by willing them to change. He willed his hair to be a different length and his face to look the way he wanted it to be. He didn't have to wash, because he could will himself clean. He could regulate his breathing and heartbeat and body temperature. He could go into a trance state, leave his body, and return to it later.

His ability to do these things came from his understanding of Martian language and philosophy. He could "grok" concepts and things. "Grok" is a Martian word meaning to comprehend in depth—knowing not only *how* something happens or operates, but also its purpose in the general scheme of things.

If Mike did not grok something right away, he would either go into a trance (especially if it really upset him with its high emotional content) or store the memory (he had a photographic memory) until he could take enough time to grok it.

When he came to some understanding of what it is like to be human—in the tragic sense of the word—and how terrible the world is for most humans, he started a church in order to help people. It was not so much a church as a Martian language school. The only way to understand Martian philosophy was to understand Martian language, which is described as sounding like "a rhinoceros ramming a steel shed." Once a person understood Martian philosophy, he could do all the things that Mike could.

In *Stranger in a Strange Land*, as in many other works of science fiction, human society is judged in the light of the fictitious standards of another planet.

Furthermore, the novel suggests that a human child can be raised by nonhumans and, though he is a "stranger" to human society, can become a superior being—capable of both adjusting to human society and making a contribution to it. This is fiction, of course. In the cases we have considered (if we can believe them), children raised by nonhumans—animals, not Martians—have never made successful adaptation to human society.

110

A recent fictional character—Lucan, on ABC television —is similar to Mike. After his early years in a wolf den, he is trained to communicate and to adjust to human life. The training is similar to the training Itard used with Victor, with one exception: the training in Lucan's case is completely successful.

Furthermore, Lucan retains certain powers that he developed in his early life—he can see in the dark, fight very well, and judge human affairs with the morality he learned from the wolves, which is superior to human's.

CHAPTER FOURTEEN

What is the Truth about Wild Children?

IT IS USUALLY not a good idea to mix fact and fiction in the same book. But in the case of wild children, fact and fiction are closely related. Kipling's story about the wolf-boy Mowgli inspired the story of Tarzan of the apes. Tarzan may have inspired the story of the African boy "John" who was supposed to have been raised by monkeys, but turned out not to have been. Many of the wolf-child stories of India are at least partly untrue, and the wolf part may have been suggested by Mowgli or other fictional wolf-children.

This might even be true of Amala and Kamala, a classic "true" case cited in many psychology books. There seems little doubt that there was *something* strange about the Indian wolf-children. Surely many of them were children who had been separated from their parents and became lost. Some of them may have been unwanted children whose parents were reluctant to kill them, but were quite willing to let them wander off into the jungle.

This is a situation that is familiar to us from our own childhood nightmares and in the story of Hansel and Gretel, whose stepmother had them abandoned in the forest. If they had not found their way out of the forest, but had survived, they would have become feral children. There have certainly been wild children. But there is considerable doubt whether human children have ever been adopted by wild animals.

There are known cases of animals adopting animals of a different species. This doesn't prove that they would adopt a human child, but it makes the possibility more likely.

On the other hand, Bruno Bettelheim, a noted child psychologist, feels that many feral children not only haven't lived with animals, but haven't even been in the wild for very long. He reached this conclusion from his experience with autistic children.

An autistic child is mentally disturbed to a very serious degree. He or she has withdrawn from the world and acts much younger than his or her physical age, with very little interest in other people. Autistic children can be extremely unpleasant to live with.

According to Bettelheim, many feral children are actually autistic. In his experience with autistic children, he has seen a clean and properly clothed child change his appearance so completely in a few minutes—tearing off clothes, covering himself with dirt and filth, snarling his hair—that he looked like a wild child straight from the forest.

Bettelheim thinks that some autistic children in poor families may have been such burdens to their parents that the parents either abandoned them in the forest or were negligent in trying to find them when they wandered off. They would not need to have been in the woods for long—perhaps a matter of hours—before they would look as though they had been there for a very long time. These children may have walked on all fours even before entering the forest. They might also act like animals in other ways.

In his special school, Bettelheim had one autistic child who looked like the perfect wolf-child. It would have been possible, like the Rev. Singh, to watch this child and conclude that the child had acquired these habits by living with wolves. But this child had never seen a wolf in his life and had grown up in the suburbs of Chicago.

Bettelheim thinks that these feral children were autistic before they left home, or they became autistic from the shock of being lost in the wild for an extended period of time. He believes that Victor, the wild boy of Aveyron, was an example of this second type.

The idea of children being raised by wild animals, according to Bettelheim, is a myth created by adults to explain why some children act so much like wild animals. For instance, reports of wild children often say that they have a very keen sense of smell. Bettelheim notes that this is also characteristic of some people with severe mental disturbance. Other characteristics of severely disturbed, nonferal children include a craving for raw food, building dens, and preferring to sleep all day. These children often bite people, as if they were wild beasts. Some of them not only do not like the company of people, but will be very friendly with dogs and other animals.

Psychologist Wayne Dennis points out that two of the usual proofs that children have been raised with wild animals are that they take refuge in animals' dens when pursued, or they are found in the company of wild animals. Dennis suggests that a child could have been found under either of these circumstances without having lived with the wild animals.

The child that goes into the animal den may simply have been trying to escape; he may never have lived there at all. Also, when a group of people are in pursuit of a child, they may drive wild animals ahead of them as well. Therefore, if a child is seen a short distance from an animal, it would seem that he is *with* the animal—but, in fact, he may not have seen the animal before. Since feral children don't talk, there is no way to ask what really happened.

116

What Is the Truth About Wild Children?

Another of Dennis' observations concerns the geographical distribution of the animals that children have supposedly been reared by. Although wolves have ranged over much of the Northern Hemisphere, stories of children reared by wolves have generally been found in India. Similarly, bears have a wide distribution, but stories of bear-boys are limited to Lithuania, Greece, and India. Dennis feels that the prevalence of a particular sort of animal-reared feral child depends mostly on the folklore of a given region.

Dennis also notes that many of the cases of wolf-reared children have General Sleeman as their source. At the time of Sleeman's travels, there were no institutions for the mentally ill in India. Many insane people were allowed to roam the countryside at will. It is claimed that when people heard that Sleeman was interested in wolf-children, they brought some of these people to him and claimed that they were wolf-children. They did this both to please the general and to trick him.

Dennis suggests that most feral children are really severely mentally retarded. That would account for their difficulty in learning to speak, their making sounds that seem to be animal sounds, their not being sensitive to heat and cold, their not caring about other people, and their difficulty in walking upright.

On the other hand, other investigators claim that retarded or mentally ill children would not be able to take care of themselves in the wild. They would not be

A nineteenth century photo of a child found in the forest of Laos. The child was thought to be a missing link in human evolution, but was obviously suffering some form of birth defect or other physical abnormality. (*N. Y. Public Library Picture Collection*)

able to learn enough about the sources of food and safe shelter in order to survive. Furthermore, a number of wild or isolated children—Kaspar Hauser is a good example—have made a lot of progress in learning and overcoming the results of their long periods away from society. What they needed was plenty of time and the right kind of teaching.

One of the interesting conclusions reached by those who have studied the cases of feral children is that if a child has not learned skills like walking upright or talking by a certain age, he or she may never be able to make up for lost time. This would explain the difficulty in teaching Kamala and Victor.

What about animals? *Have* they adopted human children? It seems likely that a baby could not survive on its own in the wild if he or she were lost before the age of two or three. Yet the feral children we have discussed were not able to speak and often could not walk properly. A child of two or three, however, *ought* to be able to speak and walk. Here are some possible explanations of these contradictory facts:

(1) the children were severely retarded or mentally ill when they were lost, yet were able to take care of themselves;

(2) the children *knew* how to walk and talk, but the emotional shock of getting lost or being abandoned caused them to lose these abilities;

(3) as infants, they were kept alive, but just barely,

119

by adults who fed them but otherwise neglected them, so they never learned to walk and talk—then they were abandoned or got lost in the wild;

(4) the children were young babies who had not yet learned to walk and talk—they survived at a young, helpless age because they were adopted by animals.

Scientists are still arguing about the correct explanation for feral children. You may or may not agree with explanation number four. The only clear modern case of a child living with animals is Armen's gazelle boy. Yet many people would feel that his report must be read skeptically; no one has corroborated his report, and there are no photographs of the gazelle boy.

Is it all folklore or fiction? Even the two writers of the book you are reading cannot agree. One believes that there probably have been cases of children who were raised by animals. The other does not. You'll have to decide for yourself.

In any case, one thing is certainly true. From Romulus to Lucan, people have been fascinated by the possibility that animals have taken care of their helpless human relatives.

Bibliography

Armen, Jean-Claude. *Gazelle-Boy*. New York: Universe Books, 1974.

Bettelheim, Bruno. *The Empty Fortress: Infantile Autism and the Birth of the Self*. New York: The Free Press, 1967.

Botkin, B. A. *A Treasury of American Folklore*. New York: Crown, 1944.

Bowman, James Cloyd. *Pecos Bill: The Greatest Cowboy of All Time*. Chicago: Whitman, 1937.

Burroughs, Edgar Rice. *Tarzan of the Apes*. A. C. McClurg and Co., 1914.

Davis, Kingsley. "Final Note on a Case of Extreme Isolation." *American Journal of Sociology*, 52 (1947): 432–37.

Dennis, Wayne. "The Significance of Feral Man." *American Journal of Psychology* 54 (1941): 425–32.

Dröscher, Vitus B. *The Friendly Beast: Latest Discoveries in Animal Behavior*. New York: Dutton, 1971.

121

Fenton, Robert W. *The Big Swingers.* Englewood Cliffs, N.J.: Prentice-Hall, 1967.

Gesell, Arnold L. *Wolf Child and Human Child.* New York: Harper, 1941.

Heinlein, Robert A. *Stranger in a Strange Land.* New York: Berkley Medallion Book, 1961.

Itard, Jean-Marc-Gaspard. *The Wild Boy of Aveyron.* Translated by George and Muriel Humphrey. Englewood Cliffs, N.J.: Prentice-Hall, 1962.

Lane, Harlan. *The Wild Boy of Aveyron.* Cambridge, Mass.: Harvard University Press, 1976. (Bantam Books, 1977.)

Lupoff, Richard A. *Edgar Rice Burroughs: Master of Adventure.* New York: Canaveral Press, 1965.

Malson, Lucien. *Wolf Children and the Problem of Human Nature.* New York: Monthly Review Press, 1972.

The New York Times. "2 Professors Rebut Report of Monkeys Raising African Boy." June 9, 1976, p. 41.

Ogburn, William Fielding and Bose, Nirmal K. "On the Trail of the Wolf-Children." *Genetic Psychology Monographs,* 1959, 60: 117–93.

Ogburn, William Fielding. "The Wolf Boy of Agra." *The American Journal of Sociology,* March 1959, LXIV, No. 5, 449–54.

Singh, J.A.L., and Zingg, Robert M. *Wolf-Children and Feral Man.* Archon Books, 1966.

INDEX

ABOUT THE AUTHORS

Lewis Gardner is a poet, playwright, editor, and song-writer. He became interested in the subject of wild children because of his interest in wolves and legends about werewolves. As a former teacher, he has also been interested in theories of how people learn.

Jack Burger's background is in the sciences, particularly geology. He has an A.B. from Columbia and an M.S. in geology from Michigan State. His scientific travels have taken him around the world by sea and to an ice island floating in the Arctic Ocean. As a geologist he is interested in finding economic mineral deposits. But it is his interest in human motivation and reaction to stress that made him become interested in feral children. He is also a writer of fiction and nonfiction and an editor. He is now working on a novel.